ASPE PAPERS:
Managing Primary Education Series

ASPE PAPER Number 4
Managing Education in Small Primary Schools

Professor Maurice Galton
University of Leicester

ASPE/Trentham Books

First published in 1993 by Trentham Books Limited

Trentham Books Limited
Westview House
734 London Road
Oakhill
Stoke-on-Trent
England ST4 5NP

British Library Cataloguing in Publication Data
A catalogue record for this book is available from the British Library.

ISBN: 0 948080 77 9

Designed and typeset by Trentham Print Design Ltd, Chester
and printed in Great Britain by Bemrose Shafron Ltd, Chester.

MANAGING PRIMARY EDUCATION

The ASPE papers comprise a series, published on behalf of the Association for the Study of Primary Education, in which major issues in primary education are analysed and implications for policy are drawn. The objectives of the papers are:

a. to shift from the inevitably reactive stance imposed by the cycle of receiving and attempting to respond to documents from bodies like DFE, SED, DENI, NCC, CCW and SEAC to a much more proactive position;

b. to undertake work on central issues in primary education which are of more than transient interest and which might be seen to constitute part of the longer-term educational agenda;

The overall theme of the first series of ASPE papers is 'Managing Primary Education'. The working titles of the papers within this theme are as follows:

Managing Learning in the Primary Classroom

Managing Teachers' Time in Primary Schools

Managing Access and Entitlement in Primary Education

Managing Education in Smaller Primary Schools

Primary Teachers, Parents and Governors

Primary Teachers: Supply, Training and Professional Development.

As far as possible the papers reflect the particular aspirations of the Association: they are grounded in careful analysis and up-to-date evidence; they draw as appropriate on school, local, national and research perspectives and on the activities of regional branches and their local groups. This range of perspectives is combined with a serious attempt to crystallise conclusions and pointers for the future.

ASPE has deliberately chosen a set of issues which are of concern to policy-makers as well as practitioners. The Association wishes to target policy makers at DFE, SED, DENI, NCC, CCW, SEAC, in LEAs, and elsewhere. It also intends to send copies to relevant members of the government and opposition parties.

The structure of the papers varies according to the theme and editors' preferences. However, the papers are intended to include:

i.   an identification of the central issues and challenges of the theme in question;

ii.   some contrasting examples of practice;

iii. reference to recent published study and research;

iv.   assessment of current strengths and weaknesses;

v.   indication of what needs to be done.

Although the papers will be published in a common format as ASPE papers, and will thus represent statements from the Association as a whole, they will also be very much the creations of their individual editors.

Managing Education in Small Primary Schools

Professor Maurice Galton
University of Leicester

SUMMARY

Evidence collected over the last decade strongly supports the view that smaller primary schools offer a curriculum and maintain standards which are compatible with those offered by larger institutions. There is no case for saying that small schools, in general, are not viable on grounds of either economic, social or curricular provision.

In more recent years informal clustering arrangements have enabled small schools to increase the range of subjects offered, improve resources and end the isolation of both teachers and pupils. The development of these clusters is best achieved when it follows a three stage pattern consisting of *initiation, consolidation* and *reorientation*. To facilitate the transition from one stage to the next requires both internal and external support teachers to use appropriate targeted training approaches.

However, recent developments such as devolved budgeting and the demands for increased specialisation as a result of the National Curriculum, may now require more formal arrangements to be established between schools within a cluster. The arrangements, called *Federations* or *Consortia*, require specific management structures to deal with matters such as, joint appointments, common purchasing policies and shared timetabling.

Legislation will be required to allow governors of individual schools to delegate some of their powers, including staff appointments, to the federation management committee. Federations should also be allowed to report test results collectively.

The Department for Education should consider funding a series of pilot projects to enable existing clusters to experiment as to the best strategies for managing these federal structures effectively.

The Viability of the Small Primary School

Teachers in small primary schools have had to work continually against a background of doubt about the viability of such institutions. This doubt has, in the main, arisen from three kinds of criticism, the first of which asserts that, because of their size and the limited number of teachers, such schools find it difficult to provide the necessary range, balance and depth of curriculum when compared to larger schools. As a result of these limitations it is further suggested that standards of performance of children in small school are likely to be lower than in larger ones. Such differences are said to be exacerbated by the wide age range and therefore ability within any one small school classroom.

A second kind of criticism concerns the possible social limitations of small primary schools, in that, so the argument runs, they contain too narrow a mix of children and therefore provide fewer opportunities for pupils to broaden their experience. The third kind of objection centres around the economic viability of small schools in that the cost per pupil is much higher and then provision of special purpose-built facilities, such as a hall for P.E., Drama and Dance, escalates these costs further. The smaller number of pupils means that, invariably, there will be lower teacher/pupil ratios and a need to provide specialist help to cover areas such as Music.

The problem in dealing with each of these criticisms is that, until recently, it has been very difficult to obtain any empirical evidence to test the validity of the arguments. A major difficulty arises when seeking comparative data because, since the inception of the primary school, the definition of what constitutes a small school has continually changed. For example, the Hadow Report (1931) gave special attention to rural schools. The report examined three examples of good practice; one with a single teacher and twelve pupils, another with one teacher and twenty-one pupils and a third with one teacher and thirty pupils. The report implied that such schools were fairly typical examples. By 1961, however, the Ministry of Education in a report entitled 'Village Schools', describes as a typical example, a school of around fifty pupils divided into two classes (Ministry of Education 1961). It would seem, therefore, that in the post war period, following the 1944 Education Act, many of the one-teacher schools in rural areas had been closed.

Concern about the viability of small schools therefore shifted to those having two teachers, since the Ministry of Education (1961) document laid great stress on the facilities which such schools should contain. They required a library area capable of housing up to fifty books, together with workshop areas for making and constructing large maps, charts and friezes, a place for physical movement so that pupils could climb ropes and ladders, practise with balls and dance to music. In addition, an area should be provided which allowed the construction of some form of portable staging so that the class could do dramatic work. Few rural schools at that time could meet the Ministry of Education's (1961) planning specification.

Further criticisms of two teacher schools arose as a result of the recommendations of the Plowden Committee (1967). Their report argued that schools with an age range of five to eleven should usually have at least 'three classes each covering two age ranges' (para 480). This would suggest, as a minimum figure, around 100 pupils and three teachers for an all-through junior and infant school. In the context of this discussion, the report noted that in 1947 there were nearly 9,000 schools with 100 or fewer pupils on the roll but that the figure had been reduced by nearly a third by 1965. Noting the faster decline of schools with fifty or fewer pupils, the report approved this trend arguing that 'It is the smallest schools which are least defensible both financially and, except in special circumstances, on educational grounds.' (para 260)

Plowden's criticisms stemmed from a view that primary schools should embrace a broad curriculum which was sufficiently varied to ensure that the needs of all children were met. According to Plowden, no one teacher could possibly be equipped to meet these demands. The report therefore suggested that staff should pool their expertise in order that different teachers could provide curriculum leadership across the full range of subjects taught in the primary school. The report, having emphasised the importance of individualised instruction, which should be tailored to an individual pupil's needs, noted the additional problems which such a strategy creates for teachers when they are dealing with a wide ability range within mixed age classes. The Plowden Committee therefore concluded on both the above counts that 'Schools should be large enough to justify a staff with varied gifts and correct flexible organisation, which does not force classes with a wide age range on teachers who are not convinced of their value' (para 453). The implications for small schools in such a statement are clear. The parallel report of the Gittins Committee for Welsh schools went even further and recommended an optimum size of between eight and twelve classes for a junior school. This conclusion was based upon similar arguments to those employed by the Plowden Committee; namely the lack of available expertise among the staff and the high cost of providing resources to compensate for this deficiency (Gittins, 1967).

Since the Plowden Report this emphasis on specialisation, particularly at the top end of the primary school, has been reinforced, culminating in the recent Secretary of State's recommendation for single subject teaching in the core curriculum in the final years of junior school (DFE, 1993). The imbalance of the primary curriculum, particularly the lack of science and the over-emphasis on computation in the mathematics curriculum, was identified in a number of reports in the early eighties (APU 1981) Cockcroft (1982). This in turn led to the view in the Government White Paper, *Better Schools* (DES, 1985) that curriculum-led staffing was an appropriate way to improve the situation. The authors of the White Paper argued that each area of the 'core' curriculum should be the responsibility of a teacher with appropriate expertise. Such experts could engage in a consultancy role in support of other staff as well as taking over some of their colleagues' teaching in the upper junior school. Recognising that such a solution was subject to the constraints of finance and staffing the authors of the White Paper concluded that, except for practical reasons, the number of pupils 'should not in general fall below the level at which a complement of three teachers is justified, since it is inherently difficult for a very small school to be educationally satisfactory' (para 275).

The introduction of the National Curriculum, has now reinforced this argument. The notion of a three teacher school as a viable unit is increasingly questioned since not only does the school need to provide expertise in the three core curriculum areas but also cope with the demands of geography and history as major foundation subjects. Devolved budgeting, where the money follows pupils, has also increased the problems facing small schools since in many LEAs there is only limited protection for small units. As the proportion of money retained as a centralised resource is reduced, the capacity of an LEA to provide curriculum support in the form of peripatetic teachers of P.E. or music, to name but two examples, becomes limited. Within their allocated budgets, many small primary schools now find it impossible to meet the varied demands of individual pupils with respect to music provision in particular. As the process of devolved budgeting is extended, and given that, in comparison to the Secondary sector, primary education is underfunded (Alexander et al, 1992), the difficulties facing three teacher schools must be expected to increase and their educational viability will become a major political issue.

Faced with these uncertainties, the response of small primary schools has been varied. A few have sought to protect themselves from the possible threat of closure by applying for Grant Maintained Status. This solution, however, would seem, at best, a short term one in that the initial financial advantages must inevitably be reduced if more and more schools choose this option. Other schools have sought ways in which LEAs, through such schemes as GEST, can continue to provide additional support, secure in the knowledge that the parents of their pupils form an articulate pressure group affecting decision making at local and national government levels. An increasingly popular, if more complex response, has seen schools pool resources by forming clusters among themselves or by linking with neighbourhood secondary or middle schools.

The main aim of this paper is to examine the management development issues associated with this cluster option and to suggest ways in which such groups of schools can promote more effective educational provision for pupils. Before discussing these matters, however ,I will look briefly at the evidence relating to the existing educational provision within small primary schools to determine whether such radical changes in their organisation structure are necessary.

Performance and Practice in Small Primary Schools

The data which provides an analysis of the performance of small rural schools in comparison with primary schools in general, has mainly been gathered during the last decade. The main sources of this evidence are two studies carried out in the University of Leicester. The first, a study of curriculum provision in the small primary school, the PRISMS project (Galton and Patrick, 1990) looked at a sample of sixty-eight schools from nine local authorities. The study collected observational data relating to the various curriculum experiences of some one thousand two hundred pupils. These children were also tested at the beginning and end of a year using similar measures to those in the earlier ORACLE study (Observational Research and Classroom Learning Evaluation) which took place mainly in suburban and urban primary schools (Galton and Simon, 1980). Subsequent work at Leicester has involved an evaluation of an ESG (Educational Support Grant) scheme designed to enhance the curriculum in small rural schools. The SCENE project (Galton et al, 1991) looked at the effects of this ESG support on groups of small schools in thirteen local authorities, nearly half of whom had also taken part in the earlier PRISMS project. Currently, the same research team is looking at the effects of the National Curriculum on small rural schools as part of an ESRC (Economic and Social Research Council) project.

All these studies are chiefly concerned with the question of curriculum provision. Other examples of research, notably that carried out at Aston University by Comber et al (1981) and by Bell and Sigsworth (1987) in East Anglia, have examined the economic questions relating to the viability of small schools as well as the issue of their social divisiveness. The results of these two studies will be briefly summarised before turning to the key questions relating to the curriculum and to educational standards.

The Aston study concerned the effects of reorganisation on six groups of communities in the West Midlands. In two of these cases the researchers were able to observe the process of reorganisation as it took place. The Aston team found that the social role of the rural school, which is often held by supporters to be of key importance, depended largely on the circumstances surrounding the community which the school served. In particular, the closer the schools were to a sizeable urban conurbation the less important was the social function of the school within the local community. In these catchment areas the majority of teachers lived within suburbia and, as a consequence, took little part in rural community life. In responding to the researchers' questionnaires, many parents argued that their local school was an important meeting place for the community but nearly sixty per cent had never attended one meeting in the school during the previous twelve months.

The findings therefore suggest that unless the school is part of a relatively isolated community it is not likely to have a positive social influence upon community life. Rural isolation, however, did not appear to have a detrimental effect on the pupils' personal or social development. Nash (1977; 1978) had earlier shown that pupils in large primary schools tended to make friends from within their own social background so that the social diversity within a suburban community did not automatically mean that pupils' experiences were widened. Nash also found positive qualities among pupils attending small rural schools. Such pupils had strong feelings of belonging to their institution and greater opportunities to practise a range of important life skills, such as answering the telephone and showing visitors around the school on the occasions when the Headteacher was busy or taking the class. Further support for Nash's findings comes from a Scottish study by Forsythe (1983) where, in the Highlands, people saw their primary schools as an important and integral part of their community. The schools' main function was to promote social interaction and integration in areas where geographical features made this difficult. Forsythe found no evidence that the children experienced greater problems of adjustment when they transferred to larger secondary schools, contrary to the views expressed in the Gittens (1967) report.

Bell and Sigsworth (1987) also found that the atmosphere of a small school made the transition from home to school less traumatic compared to the problems encountered by children attending larger suburban primary schools. In particular, unlike children in the larger schools, first year pupils from small schools were able to relate to one another across age ranges with a tendency for friendships across different sexes. Children tended to form friendships according to their achievements rather than their age. In summary, therefore, the evidence, such as it is, seems to support the idea of greater social cohesiveness among children in small schools. There is little evidence that the children from small schools were significantly disadvantaged when they moved to the larger secondary or middle school at the transfer stage. Thus small schools, when working well, would appear to exert a positive influence in the development of their pupils' self concepts.

The debate about the economic viability of small schools has also been an inconclusive one, mainly because those taking part cannot agree on the factors which should be included in the 'economic equation'. Even when the procedure is based upon the Department of Education and Science criteria (DES, 1977), which stresses those elements in the costings on which small schools are disadvantaged, the figures do not always lead to a conclusion that the small school is too expensive. The Department's criteria sets the unit cost per pupil for staffing and maintenance against the cost of transport to alternative schools and the potential loss of income from the use of the school premises for other purposes. Forsythe (1983) used these criteria to investigate the financial savings derived by local authorities in fifteen eases of closure. In seven of these cases the results were inconclusive. The data become even more difficult to interpret if the costs of schooling are treated as part of the total spending on rural communities as opposed to urban conurbations. It is argued that rural communities receive around fifteen per cent less grant aid than urban conurbations although much of this additional money does not come from Education sources but is derived through various urban aid schemes and training programmes supported by other Government Departments.

A more detailed examination of these economic arguments has been carried out by Bell and Sigsworth (1987) again using the DES (1977) criteria. They calculated the spending on a sample of small schools based upon the unit teaching costs, the unit premises costs and the unit non-teaching costs (other than premises) for each child. Bell and Sigsworth reached similar conclusions to a study carried out during the research at Aston University (Comber et al, 1981) suggesting that there is a threshold figure below which costs rapidly escalate. In general, schools with rolls of less than seventy pupils showed disproportions in costs per pupil with sharply escalating additional costs in schools with fewer than twenty-five pupils. Once school size had reached one hundred the rate at which costs increased tended to stabilise. This latter figure is similar to conclusions in an Audit Commission Report (Audit Commission 1990).

As part of their research Bell and Sigsworth also carried out a series of case studies of a particular rural area with five thousand inhabitants and seven schools the largest of which had a roll of one hundred and nine and the smallest thirty-two. Bell and Sigsworth (1977) examined three options, the first of which was to create one large school to serve all the pupils currently attending the seven separate primary schools (option A). Option B retained all seven schools but re-modelled them to meet the new schools premises regulations. The third option (C) reduced the number of schools to five each with an average of sixty pupils and three teachers.

Option A had the greatest net capital costs of over half a million pounds at 1985 figures, whereas the second option had the lowest at around £217,000. However, once these increased capital costs were set against recurrent costs, including the hidden additional costs of transport which would be borne by parents, deciding between the three options became more problematic. If the capital costs were absorbed over a twenty year period and the interest payments included then differences between all three options were less than seven per cent which is generally accepted as being an allowable margin of error for such calculations. Bell and Sigsworth (1987) therefore concluded that decisions about re-organisation mainly involve judgements about the value placed upon the superior educational facilities which could be incorporated into a newer building and that the 'economic analysis' can only take us so far in answer to the question as to which set of proposals is the most cost effective. Such calculations, however, do not take into account the indirect benefits to the local community where a viable small school can often be an inducement for people to move into a village.

Curriculum Provision in Smaller Schools

In the PRISMS study (Galton and Patrick, 1990) systematic observation was used to record the opportunities that pupils had to engage in various activities. These results were then compared with earlier studies such as the ORACLE (Galton and Simon, 1980; Tizard et al, 1988; and Mortimore et al, 1988). These last two studies took place in London schools and covered infant and junior classrooms respectively.

The main findings showed that in most respects small schools were no different from large ones in terms of curriculum coverage although small schools did spend less time on 'basics' than did larger schools. Science was well represented (11%) as was history, geography and art. In some respects, therefore, perhaps because they were conscious of criticisms, many small school teachers went out of their way to provide a varied curriculum for their pupils. In terms of the quality of this provision, however, there were certain limitations in some of the schools. Much of the work was textbook orientated and highly directed. For example, in the local authority with the highest proportion of science in the curriculum, nearly sixty per cent of this time consisted of teachers talking and demonstrating to pupils. Typically, pupils in the sample of small schools investigated were engaged on tasks for which the teacher was the main resource for information and ideas. This form of teacher-directed work occupied over a quarter of the teaching time. For a further twenty per cent of the time published workcards were the source of information. Somewhat surprisingly, since many of the small schools were in rural areas, little use was made of the surrounding environment as a focus for scientific, historical and geographical studies.

There were also some problems with the match of tasks. In any classroom the curriculum tended to be defined by the dominant age group within it. For example, a nine year old pupil's task in a mixed class, with an age range of seven to nine and an average age of eight, closely resembled that of the eight year olds. If, however, the nine year old child was in a class where the average age was ten then the set tasks tended to be closer to the ten year old age group. Part of this effect arose because able nine year olds were sometimes promoted into the older class and the slower nine year old pupils kept back, but this strategy was not so widespread that it could account for these variations in the curriculum. It needs to be pointed out, however, that such effects are not peculiar to small schools, as studies of match by Bennett et al (1984) have shown.

In most other respects the curriculum in small schools was a mirror image of that in larger primary schools and this is not surprising given their staffing. A survey of teachers in small schools showed that they were similar in background and experience as those teaching in urban and suburban areas. Teachers in small schools had similar qualifications, similar ages, attended the same number of in-service activities and also displayed similar values and concerns as their colleagues in larger schools. The majority had also taught in larger schools before taking up their present post. Because of the nature of the small school, however, their teachers did work in very different contexts, having classes which were likely to be smaller and to be vertically grouped and where they had responsibility for more than one area of the curriculum.

In one important respect small schools tended not to maximise their obvious advantage in class size. Although there were fewer pupils in a small school class, this did not result in a larger proportion of time when individual pupils engaged in conversations with the teacher. While there was a greater chance that a pupil would receive an extended period of individual teacher attention this was counter balanced by longer waiting periods when pupils either queued at the teacher's desk or sat waiting for the teacher to come to their base area. This result needs to be seen in the context of the earlier finding that many of the activities were teacher-directed and many pupils depended on the teacher as the main source of information and ideas.

These findings suggest the need to study more closely the classroom practice within small schools. The PRISMS study found that patterns of pupil and teacher behaviour were very similar to that reported in studies of the larger classrooms. Typically, whole class teaching occupied 26.6% of the time compared to 12% in the ORACLE study. The PRISMS teachers also spent more time interacting with groups of pupils and levels of time on task were higher compared to other studies, particularly at times when the teacher was the main resource used. This was frequently the case in topic work including aspects of history, geography and environmental studies. In individualised tasks such as drawing, where the children often worked for long periods without any teacher intervention, there were higher levels of distraction although these were low overall compared to other studies in large schools when children worked alone in groups. When on their own, PRISMS pupils tended to talk about their work although there was a tendency for less conversation overall. On this evidence therefore pupils in small schools do work harder and experience a greater range of teaching styles than peers in the larger school.

These results need to be treated with caution, however, because of the wide variations between schools and the even greater variations between teachers within the same schools. The existence of these wide variations between schools argues, very strongly, against the kinds of generalisations which have, in the past, frequently been made about small schools concerning their ability to deliver an appropriate curriculum for all pupils. As with larger schools, there will be some small schools which are more effective than others so that each school must be judged on its merits. What the PRISMS evidence does demonstrate clearly, however, is that when small schools are managed in ways that promote effective teaching and learning, they are fully capable of matching the results achieved in larger schools. There is no self-evident case for saying that three teacher schools are unable to deliver the Primary Curriculum.

Standards in Smaller Primary Schools

Indeed, in so far as standardised test results can be used to measure the effectiveness of provision then small schools can claim to do as well, if not better, than large establishments. Early studies of attainment in small schools were confounded by the lack of evidence about the ability of the intake. Before the second world war the majority of pupils attending such schools were the children of farm labourers. Surveys in the United Kingdom and elsewhere showed that the averaged I.Q. score was lower for the rural school than for schools in the urban and suburban catchment areas. However, since the post war era there has been a marked tendency for middle class professional families to move into the rural villages with the result that the average I.Q. score of the intake is now higher than that in urban and suburban areas combined. Consequently, it could be argued that small schools should now out-perform larger schools because of their more favourable intakes. In the PRISMS study direct comparison could be made with the data obtained during the ORACLE project since the same standardised tests were used. PRISMS children out-performed the ORACLE sample in punctuation, spelling and in mathematical problem solving, particularly at the 8+ age although some of these differences in vocabulary and mathematics had been reduced by the time the children reached the age of 10. Recent data from the pilot studies of the SATS for seven year olds also suggests that small schools do well in these basic skills. However, the comparative data between PRISMS and ORACLE should again be treated with some caution because of the time span between the administration of the tests to the two samples. It could be argued generally that standards had risen over this time interval, although among critics of primary education, including both major political parties, this is not generally accepted. What can be said with some certainty is that small primary schools do no worse than their larger counterparts on these test measures.

The discussion so far indicates that well managed small schools can deliver an education which is comparable with that provided by larger schools in suburban and urban areas. Questions still need to be addressed concerning the ways and means of ensuring such effective delivery. Answers to such questions were in part obtained from the evaluation of schools taking part in the educational support grant programme (The SCENE project) which operated between 1985 and 1990. The purpose of these special support grants was to set up pilot projects in fourteen local education authorities which would 'improve the quality and range of curriculum provided in primary schools in rural areas' and 'to experiment in ways capable of replication with the means of compensating schools for curriculum deficiencies which may occur because of their size.' (DES Circular 6/84) This is examined in the following section.

Management Strategies in Smaller Primary Schools

In the ESG project the aim of improving the quality and range of the curriculum was addressed in three specific ways. First, by attempting to increase teachers' professional expertise by means of in-service training and through increasing opportunities for professional dialogue with colleagues in other schools. Second, by exploring ways of improving the supply and availability of resources and third, by increasing the opportunities for children and teachers to meet and to work together in order to overcome the possible effects of rural isolation.

To meet these specific objectives, different local authorities used different approaches. Indeed one of the interesting findings from the evaluation was that no two local authorities chose to use the money available, some seven million pounds of expenditure on the fourteen pilot projects, in similar ways. There were, however, certain common features.

In seeking to develop teachers' expertise the majority of projects used the sums available either to appoint Advisory Teachers or Project Co-ordinators, to second Headteachers and teachers from within the participant schools, or to provide additional supply cover so that teachers could visit each other and attend in-service training. Advisory Teachers were either generalists, whose main role was to release the teachers to work alongside other colleagues, or specialists who provided 'on the job' in-service training in particular curriculum areas, mainly science, technology, humanities, mathematics and expressive arts. In some cases the Advisory Teachers were also expected to act as Co-ordinators in order to arrange the various programmes for the participating schools.

Money was also used to improve the supply and availability of educational resources by either setting up special resource bases or providing additional materials for the Advisory Teachers to take with them when visiting schools. In a limited number of cases, some schools were given the money directly to spend as they wished or they were required to compete by submitting bids for consideration to the Project Co-ordinator.

A major strategy of most of the projects was to form, or in some cases consolidate, co-operative clusters of schools. The initial purpose of these clusters was to reduce the rural isolation of both teachers and children by enabling joint activities, such as field-trips, musical events and sporting activities to take place. The cluster groups also acted as teacher support groups enabling project schools to share both expertise and resources.

It was not possible, within the time available, to carry out the extensive observations undertaken during the PRISMS programme. Pupils and teachers were, therefore, asked to record their curriculum activities in the form of a diary and these were then subsequently validated by shorter observation periods during visits to the schools. However, the framework used to analyse these diary responses was based on the observation schedules used in PRISMS so that comparisons could be made.

The comparisons between the PRISMS and the ESG evaluation data showed that the latter project had been successful in extending the range of curriculum provision within the small schools. A significant proportion of observations (15% at infant level and 28% at junior level) involved some form of technology whereas in the PRISMS survey such activities had not been observed. There were considerable more science activities than in the PRISMS survey. Science now occurred as frequently as activities involving English and mathematics. While the proportions of mathematics was slightly reduced, the range of activities, particularly that involving practical work, increased as did the proportion of time devoted to history and geography. For example, in the junior classrooms, history and geography occupied 13.6% and 13.1% of the time compared to 7.1% and 3.6% in the PRISMS study. More important was the finding that these levels were achieved by combining elements from more than one curriculum area indicating that the basic skills were being applied to different contexts across the whole range of curriculum activities.

There was also considerable evidence in a number of activities that the quality of the curriculum had improved. For example, compared to the PRISMS study there was a major reduction in the number of activities where children were observed copying information without either altering, transposing or interpreting it. Pupils were seen to employ a variety of different skills when handling information with greater emphasis on construction, oracy, the ability to transcribe and interpret information though the use of graphs, maps and charts. The use of higher order cognitive tasks involving, for example, planning and classifying also increased.

The availability of a wider range of resources also led to an improvement in the ways that the children engaged in curriculum activities. In the PRISMS study the major resource for children had been the teacher but in the ESG programme more use was made of the environment, both inside and outside the classroom, of other pupils' work and of computers. The greater use of these resources was supported by the observations that pupils engaged in more first hand experience and carried out more manipulation of actual objects. The levels of collaboration between schools within a cluster enabled the purchase of larger items of expensive and specialised equipment. Whenever such purchases were made considerable amounts of use of the items was recorded. The evaluation also showed that clustering led to considerable reductions in the rural isolation of children and of teachers. Teacher support groups were particularly successful, particularly in the early years, where previously few such opportunities were on offer. In most previous cases it was Headteachers who spent most of the time away from the school and they were invariably in charge of the junior classes.

A further positive feature of the clustering was an increase in parental involvement in the childrens' activities. This usually came about because parents were required to help transport children to and from the different schools whenever joint activities were undertaken. Having provided the transport, parents often then became involved in the day's activities and this led, in turn, to regular participation back in the classroom of their own local school. There were, therefore, considerable benefits for small schools in working co-operatively. Such arrangement helped to reduce the isolation of teachers, gave them more confidence, provided a better range of resources and clearly led to an enhancement of curriculum provision both in the range of activities offered and in their quality. Not all schools participating within the ESG programme were at the same level of cluster development and one of the main findings to emerge from the evaluation was the clear link between the relationships established within the cluster and the extent to which the curriculum provision was enhanced.

The Management Development of Co-operative Clusters

The evaluation identified three important stages of cluster development. Each stage required a different supporting structure. The first stage was an *initiation* stage. Contacts between schools were often very limited involving, for the most part, joint sporting activities or the use of shared facilities for an outside visit. One example was the hire of a residential hostel for a weekend visit by the older pupils. Although each school carried out its own programme of study, there were reductions in hiring costs for larger parties and teachers were able to share late evening supervision duties.

At this stage of cluster development, decisions about the benefits of closer collaboration evolved around questions of personal cost as against the perceived worth of any new arrangements. Thus the value of a proposal to engage in a joint project, centred upon a visit to a local history museum, was judged mainly on the number of after school meetings that were required in order to plan and organise the activity. At this stage attempts by local authorities to provide specialist support were often regarded with suspicion carrying the implication that the particular curriculum area was deficient within the school. Most important was the need to provide time for teachers to meet together to discuss ideas so that generalist rather than specialist support, someone who could offer supply cover, was most appreciated.

When seeking to develop closer links, participating schools in the study generally failed to recognise that the same process of initiation had to be undergone by both parents and by Governors. Most Headteachers informed their Governors about the existence of the clustering programme but rarely bothered to explain the educational as against the economic benefits. Neither did schools make an attempt to get their governing bodies involved in joint ventures so that they too could move, along with the teachers, to the next stage of development.

The second development stage involved *consolidation*. Having committed themselves to some degree of involvement with the other schools within the cluster, teachers now set about attempting to implement the agreed programme to the best of their ability. At this stage teachers were looking for activities and materials which could be absorbed, without too much alteration, into their existing methods of classroom organisation. Any scheme of work which required them to make radical alterations to existing classroom practice was likely to be rejected. The aim of most teachers, at this stage of development, was to implement the programme as successfully as possible with minimum disruption to their existing arrangements.

It follows, therefore, that expertise from other teachers was in greatest demand so that materials and procedures which teachers could try out for themselves were readily available. Unlike the first stage, where the support required was of a generalised kind, the most successful clusters at this second stage were those with easy access to specialist help in the form of Advisory Teachers and Co-ordinators. The models of in-service training which seemed to work most successfully at this stage were, therefore, of the kind recommended by Joyce and Showers (1980) although, in practice, only a few of the schemes which were observed employed such approaches. For the most part Advisory Teachers believed that the most effective way to change practice was to work alongside their colleagues in the classroom. Observation of this strategy would suggest that it had little to recommend it at this stage of cluster development. In many cases the Advisory Teacher did little more than act as a supply, an additional pair of hands, which reduced the class size to half but resulted in little transfer of skills between the two teachers. Similar findings were reported by Alexander et al, (1989) and further consideration to the role of Co-ordinators and Advisory Teachers will be given in the following section.

By the end of the ESG project few teachers admitted that the programme had any major effect on their classroom practice. To the question, 'Has anything that you have done as part of the training within the ESG programme led you to change your existing practice?' ninety per cent of the teachers answered in the negative, saying that they found it easier to absorb the new techniques within their existing classroom organisation. Similar findings were again reported by Alexander et al, (1989). The kinds of training procedures favoured by the LEA in Alexander's PRINDEP study (Alexander, 1991) and by the LEAs within the ESG Rural Schools programme, relied heavily on the notion of the teachers as 'reflective practitioners'. Classroom teachers were expected to develop new understandings of teaching as part of an action research programme in which they learned to reflect upon their own practice in ways that enabled them to theorise about its effectiveness. In this approach the Advisory Teacher or the Co-ordinator takes on the role of a consultant and 'critical friend' rather than an instructor.

The ESG evaluation concluded that such an approach was only possible at the third stage of cluster development, the *re-orientation* stage. By this point the cluster identity was strongly established and cluster staff meetings and management meetings become a regular feature of the calendar. Strong feelings of ownership were generated leading to the conclusion that any problems were better solved within the cluster rather than by seeking help from outside from, for example, Advisory Teachers. A noticeable feature of this third stage of development was that co-ordination of cluster activity was managed from within the group rather than by appointing an outsider. Among the cluster meetings observed at this stage there was much greater evidence of reflection and experimentation and, for the first time, serious consideration was given to issues related to teaching and learning.

Instead of trying to operate within the guide-lines suggested, teachers were now more concerned to revise the programme in order to make it work more effectively in terms of their pupils' learning. In one such cluster, for example, these initiatives extended not only to the teachers but also to parents. Parents involved in technology classes were tending to offer solutions to the practical design problems generated during the course of the lesson rather than leaving the pupils to solve them independently. The cluster management team therefore set up a programme for interested parents to help them learn strategies for supporting, rather than directing, pupils' work.

In the more successful clusters, this re-orientation stage was also marked by much greater involvement of Governors. Typically, at least one joint meeting of Governors was held per year. In one case the Governors took responsibility for compiling and distributing a cluster news sheet informing parents and other influential groups of the various activities and initiatives which were taking place.

In summary, the main findings of this evaluation are as follows. There appear to be great benefits for both pupils and teachers in small schools when collaborative groupings or clusters are formed. When these clusters move beyond the point at which they engage in a limited range of joint activities to a stage where management decisions relating to the organisation and delivery of the curriculum are shared across schools, greater benefits result. This closer collaboration increases the range of resources which can be shared, enhances learning and helps to reduce the isolation of both pupils and teachers within the school.

However it is clear that the development of such clusters required careful management. Teachers, governors and active parents move through an initiation stage where, apart from a few jointly run events, coming together does little other than allow the various parties to agree a limited set of objectives for future development. Participants then pass through a major consolidation stage requiring programmes of in-service support based upon the use of coaching methods such as those described by Joyce and Showers. Finally, relationships between the staff from different schools move into a re-orientation phase where the cluster is able to initiate and support most of the work from its own resources and where, rather than acquiring new techniques or increasing their content knowledge, teachers begin thinking more critically about the most appropriate ways of teaching the enhanced curriculum programme. A summary of this management development process is shown in Figure 1.

The failure of much in-service work in the past appears to result from a mis-match between the training approaches used and the stage of development reached. Although the evaluation concerned a particular issue of implementation, namely the formation of clusters of small schools, the principles involved in the shift from initiation to reorientation are applicable to most cases of curriculum reform. As such the messages to emerge have practical implications not only for small schools but for all schools concerned to bring about improvements in the quality of their curriculum provision.

Figure 1: A framework for cluster development and curriculum support

level of co-operation	curriculum support
Phase 1: Initiation *functional contact only*	**generalist advisory teacher** *supply teacher role*
Phase 2: Consolidation *cluster focus or theme*	**specialist advisory teacher** *run workshops* *work alongside in class*
Phase 3: Re-orientation *cluster policies* *shared resources* *'corporate identity with* *autonomy'*	**cluster co-ordinator** *co-ordinate cluster INSET* *ensure evaluation* *buy-in expertise*

The Management of Small Schools and The Educational Reform Act

The effects of many changes initiated under the 1988 Educational Reform Act are still uncertain. The last five years have seen a bewildering array of policy shifts associated with no less then five changes of Secretary of State for Education, and the National Curriculum and the associated assessment procedures are now undergoing a major revision. Previous experience with the Schools Council, persuaded Kenneth Baker to create separate curriculum development and assessment agencies, but the present Secretary of State has now decided to amalgamate these institutions once more to provide greater continuity of policy. The introduction of Grant Maintained Status and the devolution of budgets to schools has placed a large question mark around the future viability of local education authorities. This shift in funding makes it difficult, if not impossible, for local authorities to subsidise curriculum developments in small schools by, for example, providing the services of Advisory Teachers to support the work of cluster groups.

Devolved budgeting has also brought considerable problems for small schools in that formula funding, based on pupil numbers in particular age groups, no longer protects the lower staff student ratios which most LEAs previously allowed to their small primary schools.

Another casualty of the reduced circumstances facing LEAs has been the demise of the peripatetic teachers in areas such as music, drama and physical education. The costs of continuing to provide such services out of small school budgets must have a distorting effect on a school's ability to offer a broad range of curriculum activity for all pupils.

Recently, the present Secretary of State has put forward, for discussion, a series of suggestions concerning the re- organisation of primary education. This would involve greater specialisation in the top junior years of schooling together with the use of non-graduate one-year trained qualified teachers in the reception and nursery year. Such proposals, if they become policy, will obviously have a profound effect on small schools. Inevitably questions will again be raised about their viability in the light of these new demands.

The research and evaluation studies described earlier, however, have shown that in the majority of small schools informal collaborative arrangements now exist whereby clusters or groups of schools co-operate on matters of shared curriculum activities and resources. These clusters have brought about an improvement in the quality of the curriculum experienced by pupils and a reduction in isolation among both teachers and children. At the same time, it was shown that when these informal links progress to a point where formal structures exist for joint decision making within the cluster, there appeared to be further advances in the quality of the curriculum delivered. In the research now being carried out at Leicester, it is clear that the development of these more formal co-operative structures has greatly improved the capacity of small schools to cope with the demands created by the implementation of the National Curriculum at such a rapid rate. It is noticeable how confident most schools were in their ability to manage the introduction of the core and foundation subjects of the National Curriculum. By allocating to various partners within the cluster specific tasks related to the different subject areas, schools have been able to incorporate common programmes of study into their individual development plans. Indeed, the challenges facing small schools, that they are unable to deliver adequate coverage of the National Curriculum, seems to have spurred on teachers in their common efforts to find ways of coping with these increased demands.

The research also demonstrated that, in comparison to large schools, very few differences could be observed in both the quality of curriculum provision and the performance of pupils on various test measures. Where such differences did occur they were generally in favour of the smaller schools although differences of social class within the catchment areas, and therefore likely differences in the ability of the intake, make it wise to treat such differences with considerable caution. Nevertheless it can be stated with some confidence that, in general, small primary schools do no worse than larger schools.

But research on primary schools, as a whole, suggests that the reasons for the equivalence in the small schools' performance, as compared to their larger counterparts, cannot all be attributed to the efforts of teachers in the smaller schools. Part of the reasons for the equivalent performance concerns the failure of larger primary schools to maximise their potential. For example, although many large schools possess a greater range of subject expertise than smaller schools there is strong evidence to suggest that the role of the subject co-ordinator in such schools has largely been ineffectual. Alexander et al., (1989) demonstrate there were considerable problems in defining the co-ordinators' roles and their acceptance as subject or pedagogic experts by other teachers.

Class teachers had 'difficulty with the new style professional relationships in the classroom which a co-ordinator personifies. Some Heads also commented that a few of their staff were unwilling to accept the validity of a teacher who does not 'own a class' (Alexander et al., 1989, p 176). It appeared that Headteachers rarely gave any consideration to the power relationships involved. Co-ordinators, who were appointed internally, indicated 'that they felt less able to develop their role precisely because they were already on the staff and had occupied a clear (and more lowly) position in the school's pre-existing power structure' (Alexander et al., 1989, p 177). As a result, many co-ordinators never operated in the role intended. Instead they found themselves acting as supply teachers enabling other staff to become involved in curriculum initiatives taking place outside the school. The main consequence was that curriculum change within schools, where co-ordinators operated in this way, was unlikely to get beyond a point where the class teacher merely 'bolted on' any new curriculum initiative on to their existing practice. In Alexander's PRINDEP project the result was fairly stark. An expenditure of nearly £13,000,000, much of this spent on the appointment of co-ordinators, failed to change practice or affect the performance of disadvantaged pupils in these schools in any significant way.

Equally important, as discussed in the previous section, was the tendency for subject co-ordinators to believe that the only way to implement change in the classroom was by working alongside teachers as opposed to imparting any form of direct instruction. This view was particularly puzzling in cases where the same co-ordinators had volunteered, during interviews, that they developed their expertise in their curriculum specialism partly through attendance at courses consisting mainly of instruction and demonstration followed by practice. Yet these co-ordinators were unwilling to offer similar experiences to other teachers in the cluster. Part of this reluctance stems from the nature of the power relationships, discussed by Alexander et al., (1989), where co-ordinators felt the need to establish classroom credibility with colleagues rather than have it assumed.

In small schools this caused particular problems when co-ordinators were dealing with Headteachers who had charge of a class. During the ESG evaluation one such session was observed where a headteacher was working alongside the co-ordinator during a science lesson. The pupils' task was to build a wall of wooden blocks and to discover its strength. This they did by rolling a weighted plastic ball down an incline to see how many turns were required to destroy the wall. The Headteacher made no attempt to ensure that pupils carried out this experiment as a fair test. The angle of incline was not fixed, neither was the ball started each time from the same position. In many cases the ball went directly through the hole already created in the wall during an earlier turn so that no contact was made with the wall. Not surprisingly the results were very erratic. Meanwhile the co-ordinator was working elsewhere in the classroom constructing smaller models of walls out of sugar cubes and icing sugar in order to test the strength of various bonds and structures. No discussion between the two teachers took place after the lesson and at no time did the co-ordinator attempt to raise the question of fair testing with the Headteacher who, it should be said, was a person with 'firm opinions'! Asked about the lesson afterwards the co-ordinator responded,

'I couldn't tell her to her face she was doing it wrong. After all she is the Head. I just hope she will see me doing things and learn from that'

The process of development during the formation of a cluster also applies, it would seem, to teachers when engaged in curriculum development or in any form of new learning related to classroom practice. Co-ordinators, therefore, need to identify the stage which a particular teacher has reached and tailor the appropriate training methods accordingly. Only when teachers have begun to move towards a re-orientation stage in their development is the process of working alongside the teacher likely to result in critical reflection of the kind required to bring about changes in practice.

In the past, large primary schools may not have made the best use of the expertise available within the school because of these weaknesses in training techniques. The introduction of the National Curriculum, however, with its emphasis on subject specialism and on whole school development planning, has given greater focus to the co-ordinator's role. This, coupled with the limited time available for introducing these changes, has shifted the balance of re-training towards coaching and other forms of direct instruction. The evidence from recent studies, notably by Muschamp et al, (1992) has suggested that this shift away from 'action research' has resulted in considerable improvements in the quality of curriculum provision. As larger schools further improve techniques of whole school planning they may be expected to enjoy certain advantages, relative to their size, over small schools, particularly in matters of subject expertise. With the current recommendation for more specialist teaching at the top end of the junior school, and the decline in support by LEAs in the form of specialist Advisory and Peripatetic Teachers, there must be a real possibility that small schools will operate at a severe disadvantage in the future. The restriction in size obviously limits the staff available with the necessary expertise.

All this suggests that the present largely informal clustering arrangements will need to be taken several steps further if smaller schools are to cope with the challenges presented by the restrictions in funding and the need for greater specialisation. In providing specialist help in areas such as music or P.E. it would be an enormous advantage if a cluster of small schools could be certain that at least one teacher member of the group had expertise in each area. This expertise could be used, not only to train other teachers to a basic level of competence but also to take specialist teaching in a manner formerly undertaken by peripatetic teachers. For teaching the core and foundation subjects to ten and eleven year old pupils, arrangements whereby teachers from within the cluster swop classes on occasions, to deal with particular topics, has much to recommend it. Some headteachers will seek this expertise from their secondary feeder school. However, there are sound arguments for clusters developing their own joint planning structures and supporting these development plans by establishing common staffing policies whereby a range of curriculum specialisms are covered by the cluster itself. Such arrangements, by establishing formal joint planning mechanisms across schools, go considerably beyond the structures found among informal clusters. For this reason they might best be distinguished from the existing forms of clustering by calling them *Federations* or *Consortia*.

Forming Federations: Management Issues

The establishment of a federation or consortium implies that formal decisions will be taken in the belief that individual schools or the group as a whole will derive benefit from their association. Among the more difficult decisions are those concerned with staffing and resources. For example, it may be easy to agree to pool funds in order to achieve better value for money by exercising joint purchasing power but more difficult to set aside funds for joint appointments of staff or to enable the purchase of equipment by one school for use on agreed terms by others. Yet these are just the kinds of decisions required if smaller schools are to compete on equal terms with larger institutions.

One of the first steps is to decide whether these crucial decisions will be taken collectively or whether they should be delegated to one or two smaller committees. Much will depend on the extent of governor involvement and how far each school's governing body sees itself as initiating policy rather than endorsing its headteacher's recommendations. However this matter is resolved, some form of constitution will be required covering the appointment of officers (chairperson, secretary) and their length of service. Other practical issues concern arrangements for convening meetings, whether decisions will be unanimous or by majority vote and whether a stand-in can attend and vote in place of an absent committee member.

Equally important are the procedures governing the day to day running of the federation. One person will be required to take responsibility as line manager dealing with such matters as timetable arrangements for joint appointments and various aspects of financial control, including authorising payments. There also needs to be an established mechanism for resolving disputes between the various parties. Such arrangements have profound implications for management development and cut across the existing culture of small schools. In some countries, for example Sweden, where federations of this kind already exist, coherence and continuity of policy is achieved by appointing one headteacher to co-ordinate the work of several schools. While limited financial savings result from replacing six heads of small schools by one, the main benefits come from the more efficient deployment of both staff and resources and the ease of management decision making.

However, it is doubtful whether, at present, within the climate facing small schools in the United Kingdom, such a radical proposal would be warmly welcomed. Given the fears of many small schools concerning the possibility of closure, local communities, particularly Governors, are naturally jealous of their autonomy and there is a marked reluctance to allow crucial decisions relating to staffing and resources to be taken elsewhere. A more feasible solution would be for heads, in turn, to take on the leadership role within the federation for an agreed period of time. The Government has made it clear that it would welcome applications from such federation's to apply for Grant Maintained Status. In such circumstances, the federations budget would then be devolved to various schools on a formula basis, with a proportion being retained to support the Central Administration and to provide limited funds for special developments.

There are, of course, many other obstacles to such a major shift in managerial responsibility. The present Education Act requires Governors to be responsible for a school and not for a federation. Structures would be required which made the management of such federations manageable by allowing schools Governors to delegate their responsibilities to a limited number of representatives on the federation management committee. Other committee structures would also be required to deal with particular aspects of the work such as curriculum, staffing, etc. It would also be sensible to allow such federations to report their attainment results by federation rather than by individual school. Teaching appointments, timetable and other matters relating to staff deployment would also be handled centrally.

Under the present system federations would not have any legal status and could therefore not employ staff directly. They would need either to arrange for the LEA to act as their agent, for which service there would no doubt be some charge, or one of the participant schools could take responsibility for salary and pension arrangements and then levy an appropriate proportion of the total cost on the remainder. It might be expected, however, that if a sufficient number of existing clusters wished to become federations the Government would legislate to remove such legal impediments.

Conclusion

To conclude, challenges now facing small schools demand some radical thinking about existing organisations, particularly the extent to which a school's individual autonomy needs to be reduced in exchange for greater flexibility in the use of staff and resources and improved quality in curriculum provision. A particularly important feature of any developments of this kind is the need to involve Governors at the earliest opportunity since they are likely to be very cautious of anything which reduces their personal responsibility. Elsewhere, notably in The Netherlands, such major innovative steps have been accompanied initially by additional financial support from Central Government. The funding is offered to a limited number of schools on the basis of competitive bidding and all bids have to comply with the Government's specification. In the case of federations the specification might be based around the various management issues set out in the previous section.

The funding provides schools with sufficient time and resources to experiment with different solutions to perceived problems. Time for discussions among staff is particularly important at the *initiation* stage of the process. Such schools then become key elements in the wider innovation process acting as sources of information and support for the second larger wave of innovation. A similar proposal to establish federations would see invitations to clusters of schools to bid for funds to develop in ways outlined in the previous paragraph. A condition of any grant would be that the federation should create management structures which encourage the joint appointment and sharing of staff, the pooling of resources, the development of a clear leadership role for an individual within the federation and the creation of a committee structure which allowed Governors to delegate to colleagues their various responsibilities for individual schools. By the end of a transition period, say two years, the federal structure would be capable of being sustained within the normal existing levels of funding.

For over half a century small schools have struggled to maintain their identity and their status. Local authorities in the past have been extremely supportive and have generally found ways of easing the financial problems associated with the small numbers of pupils attending any one school. Such support is unlikely to continue for much longer given the demise in the powers accorded LEAs. This diminution in external support is happening at a time when the demands of the National Curriculum have increased the pressures on small schools considerably. Small schools have, in the past, demonstrated clearly that they can deliver excellence. The partial loss of some autonomy seems a small price for any individual school to pay in order to maintain these high standards in the future.

References

Alexander, R., Willcocks, J., and Kinder, K. (1989) *Changing Primary Practice,* London: Falmer Press.

Alexander, R. (1991) *Primary Education in Leeds.* Leeds: University of Leeds.

Alexander, R., Rose, J. and Woodhead, C. (1992) *Curriculum Organisation and Classroom Practice in Primary Schools.* London: HMSO

APU [Assessment of Performance Unit] (1981) *Science in Schools: Aged 11: Report No. 1,* London: HMSO

Audit Commission (1990) *Rationalising Primary School Provision,* London: HMSO

Bennett, N., Desforges, C., Cockburn, A. and Wilkinson, B. (1987) *The Quality of Pupil Learning Experiences,* London: Lawrence Erlbaum.

Bell, A. and Sigsworth, A (1987) *The Small Rural Primary School,* London: Falmer Press.

Cockcroft Report (1982) *Mathematics Counts,* Report of the Committee of Enquiry into the Teaching of Mathematics in Schools, London: HMSO

Comber, L. et al., (1981) *The Social Effects of Rural Primary School Reorganisation in England,* Final Report, Birmingham: University of Aston.

Department For Education (1993) *The Initial Training of Primary School Teachers:* New Criteria for Course Approval, London: HMSO.

Department of Education and Science (1977) *Falling Numbers and School Closures,* Circular 5/77, London: HMSO.

Department of Education and Science (1985) *Better Schools,* Cmnd 9469, London: HMSO.

Forsythe, D. (ed.) (1983) *The Rural Community and the Small School,* Aberdeen: Aberdeen University Press.

Galton, M. and Patrick, H. (eds.) (1990) *Curriculum Provision in Small Primary Schools,* London: Routledge.

Galton, M. and Simon, B.(eds.) (1980) *Progress and Performance in the Primary Classroom,* London: Routledge & Kegan Paul.

Galton, M., Cavendish, S., Fogelman, R. and Hargreaves, L (1991) *Rural Schools Educational Support Grant National Evaluation Study,* Evaluation Report, University of Leicester for the Department of Education and Science, London: Department of Education and Science.

Gittins Report (1967) *Primary Education in Wales*, London: HMSO

Hadow Report (1931) *Report on the Consultative Committee on the Primary School*, London: HMSO.

Joyce, B., and Showers, B. (1980) 'Improving In-Service Training: The messages of research' *Educational Leadership*, 37, 379-85.

Ministry of Education (1961) *Village Schools*, Building Bulletin 3, HMSO.

Mortimore, P., Sammons, P., Stoll, L., Lewis, D., and Ecob, R. (1988) *School Matters: The Junior Years*, London: Open Books.

Muschamp, Y., Pollard, A., and Sharpe, R. (1992) 'Curriculum Management in Primary Schools', *The Curriculum Journal*, 3, [1] 21-39.

Nash, R. (1977) 'Perceptions of the Village School', *Research Intelligence*, 3, [1] 10-13.

Nash. R. (1978) 'More Evidence in support of Village Schools', *Where*, No.139, 189-90.

Plowden Report (1967) *Children and their Primary Schools*, Report of the Central Council for Education in England, London: HMSO.

Tizard, B., Blatchford, D., Burke, J., Farquhar, C., and PLEWIS, I. (1988) *Children at School in an Inner City,* Hove and London: Lawrence Erlbaum.

ASPE

Association for the Study of Primary Education

A national body committed to the advancement of primary
education through collaborative study and action

ASPE aims to promote:
productive professional collaboration
the advancement of understanding
the enhancement of practice
dissemination of information
independent and informed commentary on major issues

Membership Secretary:
Janet Wellings, Education Department, Shire Hall, Raingate Street,
Bury St Edmunds IP33 2AR

Background

ASPE was founded in the belief that one of the best ways to advance the cause
of primary education, and to help those most directly involved, is through
collaborative study.

Why study? The word perhaps needs to be freed of its more arid overtones. To
study, simply, is to apply the mind in order to learn and understand. Study,
therefore, is not the sole property of particular groups or institutions but can be
undertaken by anyone, anywhere. It can also take many forms, ranging from the
'pure' study of broad issues and purposes to the 'applied' tackling of very specific
practical problems. We all need to learn and to understand in order to enhance
our practice, so study in this comprehensive sense is a basic professional pursuit.

Why collaboration? The child and the teacher are at the centre of primary
education. But they need sustaining — by fellow-teachers, by heads, by parents,
by advisers, by teacher educators, by researchers, by administrators, by govern-

ors, and so on. Each of these groups can claim to be in the business, one way or another, of supporting primary education. Yet frequently they may work in isolation from one another. Too often, indeed, this separateness may lead to mutual misunderstanding and even misrepresentation. Yet they all have something valuable and distinctive to offer.

Collaborative study of primary education harnesses the potential of each of these groups in the context of shared concerns and challenges. Mutual support and co-operation benefit everyone, but most of all the child.

Following an exploratory meeting in Warwick in 1987, the Association for the Study of Primary Education — ASPE — was launched in September 1988 at a national conference held in Leeds. A constitution was approved which reflects these basic principles, and a steering committee was elected to plan the first year's programme. ASPE is now in its fourth year, building on the success of the first three.

Membership of ASPE is open to all involved in primary education. The founding conference had strong and balanced representation from class teachers, heads, advisers and inspectors, teacher educators and researchers, as well as from other groups. ASPE's success as a force within and on behalf of primary education will depend in large measure on maintaining this balance of professional perspective. At the same time, because the classroom is at the hub of primary education, we are particularly keen to have strong representation from class teachers.

Activities

ASPE operates at two levels, national and regional/local.

NATIONAL ACTIVITIES include: major conferences (national conferences have so far been held in Leeds, Bristol, Dudley and Cambridge), liaison with other national primary organisations and groups, with LEAs and HMI, and with DES, NCC, SEAC and other official bodies; production and dissemination of papers, reports and responses both to targeted bodies and through in-house and established publications.